THE MOSTON DIARIES

CALEB EVERETT

Published by Superbia Books
an imprint of
Dog Horn Publishing
45 Monk Ings
Birstall
Batley
WF17 9HU
doghornpublishing.com

This publication and the Young Enigma chapbook competition were supported by a grant from Superbia at Manchester Pride
manchesterpride.com
superbia.org.uk

Writer development, performance workshops and touring funded by Commonword
cultureword.org.uk

Part of Young Enigma,
supporting young and emerging LGBT writers
in the North West of England
youngenigma.com

Edited and designed by Adam Lowe
adam-lowe.com

ISBN: 9781907133992

INTRODUCTION

"He was a surreal writer who only ever wrote autobiographies.
An odd chap completely unfazed by failure."
'Avant Garday' – short story, unpublished, 2015

Welcome to a collection of diaries by a writer you've probably never heard of or, if you have, wish you hadn't – in which case you're perusing this slimming world's tome to see if you get a mention. Fear not, the guilty are protected but the witty are named.

My constantly neutral expression was shattered with something approaching a smile when asked if *The Moston Diaries* were available to be published. It's a lovely career-in-reverse moment, with most of my fiction and poetry remaining unpublished or scattered within through-the-looking-class anthologies. My life has, thus far, been a study in retirement. But overhearing so much above the head of Guinness froth, I've documented the periphery of living long enough for the diaries to have made a dent somewhere in a dusty corner on an internet blog. Thank you to my two readers in Milwaukee, four in Lisbon and seventeen in Merthyr Tydfil – where Prozac is clearly in short supply – my dream of being an icon for inertia is power-mincing towards the starting line.

The title comes from the high-rise cemetery of North Manchester where I was born – though reports of my birth, unlike what came after, are exaggerated. Manchester isn't all Vimto, Pankhursts and notable serial killers. In Moston, as in so much of working-class Northern England, much of life reposes in the superfluous, with bubbling chip fat and bosom-shifting gossip camouflaging all that yearns to be said but rarely is, so I've never understood how one couldn't keep a diary.

Diaries are, for me, all about the separation of work and leisure, decorated with gossip and transforming the boring into cinematic hallucination. For a gay man gossip is like a Satanic lottery win. Whispers have never featured heavily in my fragmented jottings and, whilst it isn't glittery, imaginative fiction, the diary does not luxuriate in personal dreariness – I've never had the bowel issues of someone like Kenneth Williams to pad out the pages. Think more a Poundstretcher Alan Bennett with a Grindr account on a Greggs budget.

I have endeavoured, certainly with the following excerpts (from 2013 and 2014), to celebrate the voices of those around me: ebullient entries of a feeble existence somewhere between 'Camp in the Suburbs' and 'Jack the Quipper: Disco Years'. Some names are given with an initial alone – I never bothered to find out the other letters of their names – a few names have been changed but, for the most part, all parties have agreed to air their smalls publicly alongside mine.

This chapbook is a taster of a full scratch 'n' sniff volume to be released in the near future, which will cover a decade of diaries and be separated into three sections: *The Lady Grey Years*, which takes in doing very little with confessional verbosity; *Not If You're With Her*, a love-letter to hedonism, the Arts and finding more creative ways to exist on unemployment benefits; and *She Used to Be a Top*, which is a plotless Joycean disco through love, work and loss I've refused to serialise in *Chat Magazine*.

For those who read on, muster faint praise or send death threats, I wish to extend my appreciation – just don't expect Sartre. Now, to paraphrase the marvellous Bette Davis as Margo Channing, fasten your seatbelt, it's going to be a bumpy ready.

Caleb Everett
May 2020.

The following are excerpts from The Moston Diaries *and are dragged from 2013 and 2014.*

I've forgone individual dates for such a slim volume. Location is Manchester, unless noted, and scribbles in parenthesis are intended to sprinkle some clarity for you, dear reader.

This gale-force hangover is God's way of telling me I need to find a decent Elevenses wine. Didn't get to the New Year drag extravaganza I'd been invited to – apparently Sydney Harbour Bridge and Times Square were quaking in their kitten heels at the sheer glory of it all. See from social media that I missed very little; the seasoned performers could barely summon up a regulation swish and by 11:45pm even the headliner, dolled up like one of the purple triangles from a tin of Quality Street, was scrambling to grab his civvies from the changing room after doing an ill-timed slut drop which exposed a bollock.

Instead M. and I go to the spit 'n' sawdust paradise of Paddy's Goose Pub to meet up with (my friends) Gerry, John, Gilly, Pearl, Johnny, Rick, Helen, William, Daryl, Kieron and Niall. It's riotous. Each purse-lipped queen (ages ranging from 27 to 58) clambering to topple the last on the conversational plinth. Fog horn voices, camp lisps, regal stances, impoverished charity shop drag, eyes exchanging hands under the table, hair lacquer that could bring down a Boeing 747 and enough vicious one-liners to end peace in Heaven. Pushing sixty, the ever-generous John is still, very much, hedonism poster boy, though tonight he slightly overdoes it and his eyes are facing different sides of the pub by 9pm. He's bundled into a cab home before Nicholas, Manchester's answer to a Gucci tornado, arrives and asks where John is.

"He was absolutely pissed so we sent him home," the barman snaps.

"He was *not* pissed!" Niall (with natural Joan Collins delivery) chimes in. "He was merely over-served."

Message from Donna (my sister) wishing a late Happy New Year, adding, "You're a twat. The next time your nephew is inquisitive about Father Christmas please don't answer 'what does he do when it isn't Christmas?' with 'he's a plumber' as A. has been trying to flush a Moomin down the loo since Boxing Day."

♦

Get the half-eight train back to Moston. A svelte handsome man with tattoos and a bum like a beach ball (he's the sort of person you know has a cracked phone screen without seeing it) keeps smiling at me. After 25 years feel I may have started to transmit more sexual appeal than mashed swede.

"Hey man," he says.

"Hello," I stutter, eyes ping-ponging with nerves.

"Erm, just wanted to let you know… you've got a leaf in your hair."

To be fair there could easily have been a Carmen roller in there too. My love life is summed up and I put Patti Smith back on the iPod.

Someone on Grindr, who looks not unlike Albert Einstein with lip-fillers, is giving me "career advice" – "Dear, if you want to succeed as a writer *and* have a love life you need to market yourself properly. A tan goes a long way." If this is grown up flirting, then I'm doomed – and, depressingly, it's the most interaction I've had with a man since C. and I broke up six months ago. Perishing silence suits me more than conjuring up shady suburban *Terry and June* pairings, eventually congratulating oneself with renewed vows after 20 years of iceberg silence. Still, a boyfriend would be nice until Spring kicks in – I've had the heating on Equator setting for weeks and my feet could still chill a cocktail.

The Channel 4 coverage of Richard III's body being found buried under a car park in Leicester is dramatically zhooshed up to appear like a crossover of *Time Team* and *TOWIE*, and isn't helped by scientific expert Philippa who would be more suited to presenting *How Nazi Mega-Sharks Killed the Pharaohs of Atlantis* on the Sy-Fy channel.

Reminds me of meeting a member of the Richard III Society years ago, out-of-place at a house party in Brixton, London. A dull young man with roadkill hair – looking like a pigeon who'd inherited a shirt – he expertly managed to crowbar Shakespeare into every conversation he had that night, and one imagines beyond.

"Well Caleb, always remember what Hamlet's indecisiveness cost him – so, do you want red or white wine?"

He spoke with great passion about Richard III; equal measures authoritarian and knowledgeable, and without an iota of curiosity for the mutterings of others. I see from interviews with fans of the deceased monarch on channel 4, all of whom seem not without a bob-or-two, that the uninterrupted monologue and a Phil Spector wig must be requisites for membership.

◆

Moston being, very much, frozen somewhere between the Peterloo Massacre and the spinster-hoax of fashion that was the shell-suit we still have a mineral man. He calls today with a crate of lemonade and dandelion & burdock. Always strikes me as the happiest chap anybody could possibly witness outside of a musical. He talks to Granddad about football and then tells Nan about his wife's new business venture – namely opening a tanning salon in Moston called Copper-Cabana: "She's been a beautician for years and seen Barry Manilow in concert eight times so the name made sense really."

◆

Perform at a spoken word event in Withington. J.H. does a guest spot early on – a prodigiously talented poet whose company can place you tranquil in a Japanese garden and seconds later have the mind octopus-locked in word games that would kill a beginner. Away from us, reeking of working-class ashtrays, the other spoken word performers are all a bit *Brideshead Revisited* and don't hesitate to air it in neon-nastiness. One recites a poem about how angry he was when his mum tidied his room whilst another poet is vexed because someone at Starbucks spelt her name wrong. The mass appeal of "please pity me or I will be perpetually offended" Art eludes me like sobriety.

Start my six poem set with 'The Orchestra Bitched' and end with 'Patricia Routledge Used to Live Here', both of which are songs rather than poems – the absence of a band adding nothing to my carrion delivery. (I was the lead drinker of a London-based band.) Veer away from usual self-deprecatory remarks and dive into a quagmire of queer mid-way through the set and I swear I can hear sweat patches forming on tweed when I ad-lib some cheap ditty about poppers.

A pauper's genie in a little bottle:
an ode to room odourisers

Those dearest disco sisterly poppers,
A high exempt from the grip of coppers.
Those dearest disco sisterly poppers,
Can get you ready for those with whoppers.

A dead-eyed woman, whom I've met a few times at free wine events (or art exhibitions as they're more commonly known) approaches to critique my use of the terms "queer" and "middle-class", to demonise my championing of hedonism and for being "dreadfully rude". There's nothing quite like being admonished by someone who believes not washing her hemp dress makes her some sort of Che Guevara figure. Remain stony throughout my telling off but my renowned ability to bite-my-tongue fails me and I tell her to rehearse her next attempt at being offended as "it doesn't make you look intellectual – being perpetually and professionally 'offended' is a control phrase for those who don't wish to develop an opinion and it has no right to be considered an intelligent thing to say. All in all, it makes you look as ridiculous as a goat trying to assemble IKEA furniture." Feel slightly bad even though her smiler-with-knife attack was both homophobic and classist. It's not as if I mind bad reviews in general – recall a review in the N.M.E. letters page which likened me to a "mixture of Tom Waits and Alma Cogan". The band were a mixture of confusion and anger but I like criticism, especially when I find it perversely flattering.

♦

Hear One Direction's shocking Blondie cover on the radio, whilst trying to bleach the bathroom somewhere near the vicinity of Nan-standards. I'd happily donate a kidney if it meant never having The

X-Factory dish out former Lidl employees to murder songs in the name of charity.

Gerry suggests we meet for a coffee in town. It already sounds suspiciously like one of his pub crawls but I go along with it.

"Nan! Granddad! I'm popping out for a cuppa with Gerry."

"Okay," Nan replies without raising her eyes from the top-tips of *Woman's Weekly*. "See you in 72 hours."

Within minutes of meeting Gerry, we're in F-A-G Bar, cheekily nicknamed The British Lesion because it's so claggy everyone's stuck to the floor or furniture by filth and foundation. It's the drinking equivalent of eating out of a wheelie bin… but it's cheap.

"Y' know," Gerry, abundant in both concentration and camp, informs, "we've been out drinking solidly for three months now."

"How?! We go through money quicker than a smackhead who's found a purse."

"Not. A. Clue… mayhap it's time for a week or so off partying."

I agree but get home to the news that Thatcher is dead. We're back out within the hour with Columbia on speed-dial and poppers stapled to our nostrils. Fear Gerry and I will never leave a pub again and starting to long for simple evenings spent with paperbacks and Battenberg. Still, it's nice to be introduced to the wider world after spending teenage years creased up in a wicker chair living off a diet of Oxfam paperbacks.

♦

In Paddy's Goose, Gerry and I discussing Thatcher and Section 28 when we're interrupted by a staggering moron in his 50s who splutters:

"You can't say such vile things about Margaret Thatcher – she was somebody's mother."

"The Argentinian boys aboard The Belgrano were somebody's sons but she expected all of Blighty to celebrate their deaths… What's your point ?"

Silence.

Laugh? I nearly paid for my own beer.

(Of course, she *was* a mother – to children who allegedly

didn't even visit her when she was sitting in her own Satanic piss. That ungodly task was taken up by June Whitfield.)

♦

I'm no Doris Stokes but it's becoming too easy to correctly predict the next steel-toed boot in the face surrounding Thatcher's death. Desperately need a break from the disturbing level of jingoism the media is flinging about over a vicious tyrant in brogues. A fortnight in Pyongyang should do it – must remember to pick up a fridge magnet for Gilly.

B. asks me to appear on his radio show, to talk about Thatcher and the de facto state funeral. I like B. very much though I do wish, after all his hard work, he'd stop thanking Jesus for everything that swings his way. Remember S.'s advice "try not to say fuck – and if there's a mouse in the room don't screech like a tea-kettle." As predicted, the station wished they'd never asked me. I crack some cheap jokes, comment that anybody who isn't glorifying her is being stamped as a "loony-left, vegan, Muslamic, politically correct poof" (which, of course, I probably am), then concisely compare Thatcher to Myra Hindley. They're promptly inundated with complaints and there's a radio career down the pan.

♦

Watch bits of the funeral hoping that someone will hurl themselves under the hearse, like Emily Davidson. After the funeral it's straight into *Bargain Hunt*. A stroke of genius that only gets better when one of the contestants wants to buy a cast-iron coal stove. The lady will be turning in her grave.

MAY – AUGUST 2013

Disastrous first date with Jacob and his eye-shattering Ibiza tan. Meet at 6.30pm for drinks and by 8.30pm I'm cackling with the gals in Paddy's Goose about how bad dates stalk me like a sex pest at a school on Polling Day. Jacob spoke about nothing but his gym routine but, having never set foot inside a gym, nor dated anybody who has, a six-pack to me is still something that exists for digital gays only. I'm stuck with the analogue ones. Pearl offers up wisdom: "Your prince will come, sweetcheeks. I got mine in the end. He can be a mute bastard but I love him and I'll be with him until I croak. It wasn't always so lovely though. I had to go through loads of twatwaffles before I met him. One stabbed me, another one was so addicted to ketamine and LSD that we ended up in a car crash, *another* one stabbed me and there was one who looked like Jeanette Krankie." William, on the other hand, offers his summary of dating with fantastic brevity: "Erection and rejection – *that's* dating."

I'm as shocked as Nan is when I make it home before midnight. A hot Vimto, a crafty cig now Granddad is in bed and an episode of *Hetty Wainthropp Investigates* rounds "Can't Get A Date" Night off nicely. Nan and I talk for an hour or so, her reflection-pool eyes sparkling red-brick Northern eloquence and toasty-warm humour. Grumbles that Granddad won't invest in new glasses but rather has expertly layered yet more cellotape on top of the last lot to keep them in place – "Well, I say cellotape – he's used bloody gaffer tape this time."

She falls asleep on the couch before the end of the whodunnit. I sit for a moment, perched in the mind on Varicose Lane (a sanctuary past the sun for those who fear losing loved ones), and appreciate my creaky suburban home with Nan, Granddad and (my Great Aunt) Rene. It can be lonely in a generation where people seem eager to invest in an emoji rather than an emotion but being here (even if horse-powered emotions can sometimes be under generational lock-and-key) I feel so very loved – and, of course, it's a pleasure to be around someone who can so casually talk about Hylda Baker whilst peeling spuds.

◆

Enjoying the developing friendship with Stevie and worryingly (for me) cannot imagine a life without him. Though we met on a date we've quickly become sisters rather than misters – though also something beyond either. With his cherubic face of thunder and a stature so petite he looks like a handsome paperclip, it's easy to place his age closer to teenager rather than mid-20s. Some clearly think he's *much* younger, as I find out at dinner when a waitress minces over to collect my empty plate, turns her head to inspect Stevie, then back to me to say, "Awww, still going at his pizza is he?" A father to a 23-year-old at 25! Still, it drives me to drink so I can't remain upset – and, like bitches of a feather, it's impossible not to cackle with Stevie who minces everything but his words. Get home and instantly shave the beard which takes a fortnight off my forever jet-lagged face.

♦

Rejection email from [A "Queer Art" Festival] informing, after some praise, that my play is "too radical, too left and too queer". It sounds like a satirical version of the vicious "no Irish, no blacks, no dogs" signs that would hang outside 1950s B&Bs – alas, it isn't. Day is brightened, slightly, when P.W. contacts to say, "I was watching the news earlier and there was a piece about someone in Idaho who had gone missing. Their 'missing photo' had been placed on milk bottles and they've been found alive and well one state over. It sprung to mind that in the case of you they'd have to do it on bottles of poppers."

Obsessed to the point of excavation with (the artist) Edward Hopper. His paintings are cutting, without being sentimental, because of the impenetrable silence; space between people was *everything* and, much as I've adored his work, find I can talk very little about any paintings I like when around them. It's a sense of studied awe, similar to how I felt gazing at the Rockies or The Grand Canyon (I ran away to America in 2004) where I'd need a decade in a Tibetan monastery before any words worth speaking could tombola from the lips. Something similar happens in the company of overly beautiful people. Anyone with a healthy mixture of self-esteem issues is far more at home with stomach-turners than head-turners.

David Lynch is obviously a fan of Edward Hopper and I go straight back to watching his möbius strip mistresspiece *Inland Empire* – whoever edited that film has to now be living in a gated community in Florida with 24-hour care.

At 7pm I go to the local chippy for Nan, Granddad and Rene's supper. Put in my order and wait outside to smoke. I'm propositioned by a woman in her 40s who looks every inch a cartoon of prostitution-in-fishnets wearing a wig that would make Terry Wogan wince.

"Looking for fun tonight? £30 and I'll go all the way."

"Erm… no, sorry… I'm gay."

"Well, we can all do with a night off."

Though there's truth in that, I go back inside the chip shop to wait for my order. Mrs. Wong (the owner), who has known me since I was 7 and still offers me a singular chip on a wooden-fork as "a little treat" whilst waiting for the food to cook, asks, "Has she been offering you bootleg DVDs too?! Right, I'm off to shift the cheeky cow." I don't correct her assumption.

♦

Gerry and I end up out for a one-drink weekend and the diary disintegrates like a frail cream-cracker in the mouth of volcano. It's "bitch, bitch, bitch" then, for a bit of a rest, "vile". What wonderful sisters we are. Venture to Company (a men-only bar) which resembles a methadone drop-in centre for bears. A tall Irish chap starts chatting me up. Startled into silence by such a rare occurrence Gerry takes it as an opportunity to go and cruise in the toilets. The Irish chap quickly loses interest and balance is restored, so I dance and await Gerry's return from his cistern love. Ten minutes pass, then fifteen. At the 20-minute mark two men from behind the bar rush into the loo with undisguised panic. Moments later they're carrying out an avalanche in Ralph Lauren of a man who looks rather unwell. Then Gerry appears, shaky legged and ashen faced.

"Are you okay, love?"

"No, gurrl."

"What's wrong?!"

"Well… I was in the cubicle with some fella. He was having a go and he… well… he had a stroke."

(Holding in so much laughter I'm fearing a hernia) "My word! This just happened?"

"No, gurrl. It happened about fifteen minutes ago but he was too fat to move from the door… I had to do an SOS with loo roll over the door."

"I've heard of a dick-of-death but that's ridiculous."

♦

So poor I can barely afford biros from The Works these days. Start applying to take part in paid market research studies and hear back from one almost immediately and, if I can make it today, I'm to be quizzed about television for an undisclosed company and receive £60 to talk for 45-minutes (they'll wish they never asked.) I attend, I am given a cup of tea, and the interrogation begins. After 15-minutes the lovely lady hands me £60. Remark I'd been told it would last longer (story of my life) to which she replies, "Well, you've been very articulate, are very bright and you've covered more than we had even hoped for." With that I get up, feeling rather pleased with myself, and proceed to walk straight into a glass door.

♦

Casting rumours about Rolf Harris being the latest star to join Operation Yewtree are confirmed. What with Germaine Greer being loathed for her supposed anti-trans stance, Australia are putting a lot on the padded shoulders of Kath and Kim.

Manchester is battered with sun. Met Jess for the *Coronation Street* tour she's booked us onto. Though both depressed just a day ago we're all tits 'n' teeth. Jess is once again on her shift-without-end, namely "humourist as sharp as a light tasering". Her mild infatuation with a local barista has come to an end so we're back to having a crack at putting the celebrate into celibate. Decide to get a little stoned before joining what is clearly a remarkably inclusive tour, as there's a gathering of blue-rinsed OAPs *and* felt-hatted OAPs outside Bootle Police Station ready to start the tour. A man dressed in a waistcoat the colour of cat-vomit and with arms like an old quilt shoves past Jess and me, without apology or eye contact. He declares himself tour guide with booming 1950s theatre delivery, "For those with Zimmer frames, fear not – we won't be walking too far on this tour and, obviously, we won't be going anywhere near Coronation Street or its sets."

Jess and I cannot decipher the sense from the stoned and so don't question the pivotal but missing-in-action aspects to the soap opera safari. The tour guide starts by telling us Bootle Police Station was where John Savident (who played butcher Fred Elliot on the show) gave evidence, after a rent-boy attacked him a few years ago. The surrealism stakes are upped.

"Mr. Savident met the young man in a bar in Manchester's Gay Village. He asked the man if he wanted to come back to discuss the theatre – now, for those who don't know, nor would I expect you to, in gay parlance the question 'would you like to come back and discuss the theatre?' actually means 'would you like to come back and engage in sodomy?'"

For a moment Jess and I are stunned into stoned silence, then erupt like hyenas on helium and are ordered to "shush or leave". We leave. Still can't quite believe the antiquated vocabulary of the tour guide – but then that's probably rich coming from me.

Get home and start dismantling my bed in preparation for the new one arriving tomorrow. Find an unopened packet of cigarettes, a shirt I'd assumed stolen by tracksuited trade and an anonymous Valentine's Day card I got through the post years ago in which was scrawled "you're a cunt!"

◆

F. contacts to say he's got a new job and perhaps we should start looking for a place to live together soon but F. has a talent, second-to-none, for getting fired. For serenity I'd rather be lodging with Anne Frank.

Meet Adam for cheap wine and cheaper tales of sex. Bump into two local queens we christened The Golden Shower Girls years ago. One complains about pulling a calf muscle during an orgy last night. Never understood how people actually meet people so orgies remain as mythical as centaurs to me. If I could blush I would but, unflustered and considering dry cleaning bills, ask, "What do you do *after* an orgy? I can't look a barman in the eye when ordering a porn star martini."

"Well most of them were playing butch so they put *Die Hard* on the TV. Me and her went into the other room and watched *Hocus Pocus*."

Adam tells me he's thinking of a "one-man show/installation called *Literary Prostitute*. You'll be the writerly whore – people can book you for dinner or a day out; they can drop into a bar to share their fantasies and yours! Essentially you do your storytelling street-walk in killer heels. It'll be produced by me, naturally." Sounds very Quentin Crisp and I'm rammed to the flaps with joy. Hoping this comes off as all I've wanted is life to be kind enough to keep me waged *and* tipsy.

♦

In Liverpool to meet C. We discuss the possibility of doing some recordings in October. Within minutes of arriving he's ironing out arrangements for "Apathy in the UK" and "Little Stoned Eyes" breaking only to giggle to himself then remarking they're "like the work of a scally Noël Coward" – which is a shiveringly sweet thing to hear.

After a few hours of work C. and I attend Dan's gig (a friend's new band, in which he plays guitar). Have to flee the crime scene after four ditties because the crayoned-in-tribal-tattoos singer – who spends most of the night singing in the key of Yale – flicks his locks, winks at someone near the stage, dedicates the following number to them and proceeds to screech into a version of "All You Need Is Love" so updated that he managed to remove notes altogether. Leave during an acoustic number he's written "in response to war". Most people have a song or two in them but, in most cases, that's exactly where it should stay.

On the train back to Manchester thinking of my life in London a few years ago. Miss having a band but not entirely sure I would want to be in one again. Not because of a lack of interest but rather for the same reasons I no longer watch soap operas – I'm afraid of the commitment.

SEPTEMBER – DECEMBER 2013

Involved in something of an unexpected romance with A. Though a few years younger than me, he's a fogged train-station old soul who can reduce me to ab-aching fits of giggles and he sports cheekbones of unscalable bluff. Nan approves with a remark about "how handsome and tall" he is, followed by a mischievous wink.

A. and I spend most of the day watching the wonderful old films *Brief Encounter, It Always Rains on Sunday* and *The Ladykillers*. Break for an intermission and end up wandering around Moston cemetery which itself seems to have been roused from an Ealing comedy, as we see weather-beaten 19th Century headstones that read "Queenie Allcock", "Fanny Lynch, Spinster" and a rather pathetic terracotta pot with the simple engraving "Rest in peace May. From all your colleagues at -". Without even a surname, we decide it wasn't that May was particularly disliked but rather shy with a case of halitosis so severe it could scorch furniture polish, so her colleagues didn't bother to get to know her. As serious as a good haircut we decide we'll buy flowers for her tomorrow.

A. asks me about death and tell him I've had my epitaph ready since puberty – "Here rests Caleb Everett – Your Loss."

♦

I meet Nan in town (I'm now living in Hulme). She wants to do some shopping for the tedium of birthdays and Christmas to come. We're in The Card Factory. Nan needs some glittery numbers to stick on the front of birthday cards, just in-case the recipient has forgotten – or is trying to forget – just how old they are. There are two women, clearly mother and daughter (in their 50s and 30s, respectively) looking at packs of glow-in-the-dark balloons. The mother speaks, "What a bloody stupid idea… I mean, when was the last time you gave someone a balloon in the dark?"

Nan and I go into The Moon under the Water for a bite to eat and a drink. Stunning building – a former theatre but, as with most Wetherspoons, they turn bomb-shelter-British-glamour into little more than chip-fat migraine aromas with a drinks menu that's just a ketchup-stained lobotomy with a price list. An elderly space-hopper in a tracksuit rolls over to Nan and me and endeavours to spark up a conversation about "fucking immigrants". The wonder she is, Nan shuts him down very quickly and he rolls away deflated. As with most racists, his birth looks like the result of Bernard Manning ejaculating into a mouldy bucket of KFC and he sounds like he gets his news from a drunk man riding a horse.

Nan is on fine form and reels out stories of her days behind

The Old Loom (a pub in Moston). Like most pubs of its time The Old Loom had two separate rooms: a vault for the men and the lounge/snug for both women and men to sup up in.

"There was an Irishman who fell into the vault one day. Bumped into two tables before he reached the bar – and the bar was closer than the tables. Anyway, I told him he was too drunk and he said, 'Ah, that's fair enough, me love; fair enough.' He wandered out of the vault and straight into the lounge so I just crossed the bar and said, 'Sorry, love. Like I said, you've had a bit too much today,' and he said, 'Oh, I don't feckin' believe it – barred from two pubs in two minutes!' Right Honeybun, I best get back – there's bacon in the fridge for your Granddad that needs using up before midnight."

♦

The news is just an exercise in torment. After five minutes all I desire is to pen a power ballad and drink myself out of oblivion. Staying with Gerry at the moment, where we have more poppers in the fridge than food. Try and reclaim the muddled memories owned by last night's drinking but remember nothing after the second trip to buy (the over-the-counter legal high) Ching which, as a drug, is a dancefloor God-Complex in an abandoned car park.

"Oh gurrl" Gerry's eyes widen as memories interrupt hangover. "Last night we bumped into that horrible bearded queen who stole from you."

"Did we?"

"Yes, you were coming up and hugging everyone – it was disgusting. Then she minced over to try and dance with you."

"Did he?"

"You hugged her and said, 'I'm on a drug that makes you love everyone and I still think you're an insufferable, nasty, bullying hag.'"

"Did I?"

At this rate I really am stuck with the friends I've already got – not that I wish to procure any more.

Adam contacts us both to say he's looking forward to recording an interview we're doing later for some LGBT exhibition next spring. We've no idea what it entails and assume it was agreed to when drunk, thus incapable of saying "no" to anything. Gerry talks eloquently about dance, HIV and poetry. I witter on about Quentin Crisp, camp and Polari. They seem pleased but in a time where gay men have seemingly cut out the middle-man where homophobia is concerned and camp is demonised to the point of disease, I doubt I'll make the exhibition.

◆

Lou Reed has gone up to the sky. Often attracted to "unconventional" singers and the first few years of his career mean as much to me as freedom to a caged bird. Visit N. and D. in Liverpool and The Offbeat Generation are reunited. Go to The Egg Café, chat about Lou Reed/ Velvet Underground and Nico – who lived in Manchester during the late 80s. (A friend of mine witnessed her refused from a glitzy afterparty in 1986, as the bouncers mistook her for a vagrant.) All cups of tea freeze between table and mouth as we gawk at a middle-aged lady who, eating spaghetti, proceeds to wind it neatly around a fork, then retrieves from her handbag a pair of compact nail scissors. She proceeds to trim the spaghetti dangling from her mouth and then chew with remarkable composure. Lovely day.

N. and I spend the evening in a pub (Ye Olde Cracke), where John Lennon performed with his first band. The wooden tables are not expensive pieces trying to look knackered – they *are* knackered.

Meet a rosy-faced old drunk who tells us why the snug is called The War Room: "When I was your age we'd have all the old guys who wanted to sit down and talk about the war, in peace and quiet – away from our loud bloody music – so they gave the old guys this room. Now I'm one of the old guys and I prefer this room to talk about the racket *we* made."

Get home and call A. He tells me he is relocating to London in a week or so. Cannot follow but we agree to stay in touch. Glumness sets in and I note the life of a gay man isn't all glitter – there's always the darkness of loneliness looming or, worse still, that someone will contact informing you it's your turn to marry Liza Minnelli.

◆

My 26th birthday. Receive so many beautiful messages I feel like a walking condolence book to Princess Diana. I'm already considered to be much older than my years on the gay scene – there are numerous reasons for this, none of which seem to be because I look like dust in mascara. I suppose some people are simply meant to have friends rather than a list of failed relationships. Meet Stevie, Gerry, Jess, Maria, Ben, Scott, Dan L. Adam and Gilly in Paddy's Goose. Others join and there seems too many people for it to be my party.

Dan L. was hysterical – only 24 himself but complaining about looking older than his years. "I don't judge my age by old face pictures anymore. I judge it by pictures of my arse."

Camp doesn't take maturity with any seriousness – it's a lifelong pose that treats the act of boarding a bus like it's the QE2.

♦

Bus into the shitty centre to meet Stevie. The weekly tickets now come printed with the name of a vegetable at the bottom of them. Apparently to combat fraud, as people were printing their own. Oh, Manchester. Today's vegetable is "pepper".

The howling wind styles my quiff into Ronnie Spector's beehive. Not complaining but it's too cold to loiter and there's no point suffering for beauty on a deserted street. Head into a pub for a green tea by a roaring fire – damn arsonists – to wait for Stevie. A youngish man (though younger than me) is discussing Syria with a slightly younger woman.

"Well, what I say is just bomb the fuck outta 'em. I'd feel much fuckin' safer going 'round the Christmas Markets."

I haven't the patience nor the crayons to tell them how wrong they are so wait at the bar for Stevie.

♦

Appointment with my GP after yet another horrible throat-infection that has left me sounding like Bonnie Tyler playing Darth Vader (Martha Vada). Dr - asks if I smoke. One should always treat a doctor like a confession booth so tell her I do indeed smoke.

After five minutes of mildly appreciative but histrionic finger-wagging she matriarchally whispers, "Well, that's your telling off – now, let's get to know each other whilst I put through these appointments. What do you do?"

21

"I'm a writer."

"Oh… in which case disregard everything I've just said – you'll never give up smoking."

Howl with laughter and she books me in for an ENT appointment in February. Utterly charming lady.

◆

Making the most of my seasonal blues voice, Gilly and I end up performing at Paddy's Goose with a keyboard player. Me on harmonica and occasional croaks with Gilly and L. (the keyboard player) sharing vocals. I sing Muddy Waters' "Mannish Boy" – Mississippi masculinity replaced with a gruff Bea Arthur impersonation but it seems to please a cauldron of creaky queens.

An elderly drag queen in a Bo-Peep gown (and on so much speed I nickname her Gram-Ma) is ogling the stage with volcano-erupting determination. I go outside to smoke whilst Owen (the barman) tries to rugby-tackle her from storming the stage for a surprise striptease. Having witnessed this once before I have no need to gawk at varicose high-kicks to Kylie Minogue by legs that wouldn't fit through the Suez Canal, all the while Gram-Ma tears at Primark underwear to expose that which would make the blind thankful. Still, I admire her inability to be timid. Outside I end up chatting to a woman in her sixties who is the size of Sooty and caked head-to-toe in QVC jewellery. She describes herself as being like "Mrs Overall in a porno" and commented on the demise of her fourth marriage, "He said 'I'll have to show you how to wash pots,' so I washed 'im outta my life." She disappears not long after this without Gilly or Stevie having clapped eyes on her, so I naturally assume she was my spirit animal summoned by a harmonica in the key of C.

JANUARY – APRIL 2014

At J. and D.'s for dinner. Not known for accepting invitations for solids, preferring my menu in a glass. As the weathercock wit Brendan Behan quipped, "I'm a drinker with a writing problem" – I've managed, for years, to survive entirely on nutritional supplement drinks designed for seniors, and the moisture in the air. Should I ever enter the world of rap my stage name is already earmarked as Complan B.

It's the usual pantomime-sister's run-through of gossip with J. and D. It's all highly enjoyable but J. has a habit of 'she-ing' *everything* which can, occasionally, make language as sturdy as scaffolding made out of playdoh. It gets all too much during the main course when J. says, "She's a good do, her – so she is."

"Who?"

"*She* is!"

"Who?!"

"The gravy, dear – the gravy!"

"*Please* luv, don't 'she' the gravy."

After dinner I'm more at home, sherrying and socialising. There's a fascinating woman called M. who has manoeuvred herself from florist to manager of a swinger's club to escort to comedienne, all before the age of 40. She flickers with 1950s radio broadcaster charm and by gin number two she's dished out so many elaborate and detailed anecdotes about former punters the other guests have given up blushing all together. M. has a larger frame which was, she says, her "main selling point".

"Oh yes Caleb, when I was over 20-stone I'd have men queueing for me to sit on them. It's called 'squashing' – I'd just sit on them eating pizza and watching TV."

"So they'd turn Smurf-blue, you'd get up and have made how much, if you don't my asking?"

"Between £500-£1000."

"Did you ever charge rich people more?"

"No – but I would have charged more if you could tell over the phone who voted Tory. I'll have to send you some links to my reviews on PunterNet."

I do admire those who treat life as an honest and witty open diary – it's pivotal for happiness and it weeds out the blackmailers. All in all, a nice evening and trumps the last dinner party I attended, at which a student with more piercings than IQ points (and believed himself to be clairvoyant) cornered me to spill his vast body of collected traumas and allergies. My morbid fear of boredom was shattered only when someone opened a packet of dry-roasted peanuts which instantly sent someone into anaphylactic shock. The charmless clairvoyant remained silent until the ambulance arrived. He'd clearly never seen

Abigail's Party or enjoyed himself without rushing to the confession booth of a blog.

♦

Hospital appointment for this throat infection which resolutely refuses to budge. Medical problems, no matter how trivial or severe, are as boring as sin. Though for writers with an ear finely tuned for a Northern soundbite it can be a sterilised Aladdin's Cave.

Arrive fifteen minutes early for my appointment at 10am. Another waiting room and another bead-maze-table-toy I must resist playing with. Two elderly ladies do a crab-like shuffle to the seats facing and scan the announcement board on the faded shade-of-dull wall behind me. One of the felt-hatted dears taps her companion on the arm.

"D' you know what I thought that said? I thought it said: 'Are you tired of Domestos' abuse?' I thought, 'Funny thing to have a helpline for.'" Alan Bennett would kick off his court shoes, peel the cellophane from his sarnies and prepare for a long stay but I'm called in by the nurse.

Older Nurse: Hello luv. Come in and take a seat.

Me: Thank you.

Older Nurse: Goodness, your throat is very hoarse, isn't it?

Me: I know I sound like Deidre Barlow now but it's better than a fortnight ago… I sounded like an asthmatic Phyllis Pierce.

(Nurses laugh but the younger nurse is clearly baffled by the latter name.)

Older Nurse: She won't know who that is. How do you know who she is? That's way before your time.

Me: I was dragged up in the dressing rooms at Granada so I can natter, from arsehole to breakfast time, about *Coronation Street* from decades before I was born. Especially Pat Phoenix, who has the greatest opening line to a memoir ever – 'I am a bastard.'

Older Nurse: *Coronation Street* would have to be my specialised subject on *Mastermind*. I still love it but it was much better in my day, before everyone was killing everyone over having an affair.

Me: Definitely. The women in it are so poorly written now. No high hair. No ambition beyond a deep-fat fryer. They're just constantly weeping over some man who resembles a tin of spam with a beard. I mean, who'd want to drag up as any of the women in it now?

(The older nurse and I exchange stories about favourite monochrome soap moments.)

Younger Nurse: Ooh, I've got a claim to fame with *Coronation Street*! You remember the guy who played Jack Duckworth?

Me & Older Nurse: Yes.

Younger Nurse: Well… he's buried next to my granddad.

Issued with a follow-up appointment for next week, when a camera will explore the throat properly. Until then I'm to speak as little as possible. Feel a popular week ahead.

Feeling mortified, just like a good lapsed Catholic should. Earlier today Nan let the golden skinned window cleaner, Daz, in to use the loo. He's a tracksuited Triga porno dream. Gold chains, bad tribal-tattoos, Christmas Lynx aroma and knockoff flea-market sportswear, which makes him look like a sexy living barcode. He's all anyone could ever want to fill the lonely hours between *Jeremy Kyle* and *Loose Women*. Moston's own George Formby with an ASBO, ready to treat his lover to 3-for-£5 Blue WKDs after his window cleaning round. I'm unaware Daz is in the house as I'm bundled in the shower. The windows were cleaned ages ago so I've no reason to lock myself in a coffin to avoid drooling over a scally with a shammy. Daz uses the toilet and strides over to the bathroom. Just wrapping myself with a towel, the door opens (dodgy council-fitted lock) and in pops the Adonis in Adidas, not in the least bit embarrassed.

"Ah sorry mate. Just need to wash me hands. Good job ya got a towel on, eh?" He laughs, which thankfully muffled the sound of my ovaries sighing. In a somewhat dazed state, I reply, "I would've trimmed if I knew I was going to have company." A half-smile of pity for someone tranquilised in sexual quarantine and he flees, leaving me mummified in a cotton towel.

Away for the writer's course, kindly paid for by [a local publisher]. Clearly there are some individuals who wish this brooding anti-matter would talk less and write more or just do either out of view of the ever-growing beehive of Manchester's skyline. It pleases few that I'm constantly referring to the writer's course as a "holiday". This could be because the other writers, most of whom are likely paying, are hoping workshops will hone their skills and regimented routines will induce an easier time of being a writer. For their sake, I hope so. For me writing is the rehearsal for reality. It's also a very physical exercise that can leave one sweating myopic fluid – even if it's the only exercise that'll result in one's body resembling a cushioned dog's bed. Perhaps it's why so many writers turn to mindfulness and yoga just before tumbling into irrelevance. I'll stick with minefield-ness even if relevance never kicks the backdoors in for this mendicant scribbler.

Pass through Hebden Bridge and Heptonstall to Lumb Bank, the former house of Ted Hughes and Sylvia Plath. As wild inspiration goes, it's hard not to wear out a biro within seconds of sitting in a room where Plath more-than-likely called Hughes "an overrated twat". No television, no radio and no cages. Bunnies binky through greenery; the likes of which were banned from Manchester after Piccadilly Gardens was ripped up and replaced by a concrete pigeon zoo where it is impossible to steal a second of happiness. Not even in the Greggs there will the workers crack a smile and they're cheery everywhere. The scenery outside Lumb Bank is enough to send any artist swirling towards the nearest daffodil to croon but it simply relaxes my soul, and I sit for what feels like a blissful eternity before I realise the other writers are finger-tapping in a different room, waiting for me to join. Greet the six other writers, all of whom are gay, lesbian or bi-standers. Pervasive feelings of fraudulence tap-tap-tap the grey cells – always happens when around writers who twinkle with fiction and are riddled with work-ethic. Within minutes I'm terribly fond of them all but it's Allie and Jane who steal my heart. Allie, all fidgety nervous hands when speaking, is an elfin spirit whose glasses I can never imagine steamed up by rage and her oversized gabardine jacket never anything other than pristine. Surprised to find she's over a decade older than me, as time has demanded nothing from her face and she could pass as billboard material for a teenage shampoo commercial. Jane's enunciation is blasé royalty and nobody dares to ask her age (likely to be somewhere in the mid-70s). She looks not unlike Germaine Greer minus any window-frosting glares. The two course-leaders enter the living room – one of whom is (my friend) Jonathan K., whom I've not seen for 6 months or so, and Kerry H., whom I've never met and holds herself like a never-to-be-claimed trophy.

"Caleb, I didn't know you were doing this course. I didn't know you did courses," Jonathan says in that way of his where anything sounds like it's drawn from a 70s risqué celluloid trip, handle-bar moustache included.

"I don't usually but Manchester deserves the rest."

By 8pm, wine that tastes like the sweat of the antichrist is flowing Kerry askes each writer what they wish to "gain from the course" – "I'd like to work towards improving my dialogue in short stories," "I'd like to improve my descriptive abilities," and so forth. It gets to me and, happy with my own limited style, say without thinking, "I'd like the weather to stay lovely and visit Trades club in Hebden." Bewildered looks, wondering if this jelly baby on growth hormones is arrogant or just dim enough to have a column in *OK Magazine* – but Jane leads in chortles. Then she shyly remarks, "I'd like to learn how to swear." More bewildered looks, now with me as lead drinker of arched eyebrows. "You see in all my years I've never swore. I'm writing a memoir about my time in a convent and being sent to Harley Street to 'cure' me of falling in love with another woman," more than just a sprinkling of heartbreak and regret in her voice, "so I'd like to learn how to swear – both on and off the page… and be a little more assertive by the end of the week." The heavens target me with a reason for being here and I promise to have her cursing like a Navvy within 48 hours. (It took a lot less.)

◆

Wake to the devastating news that my red-wine co-conspirator Scott M. is dead, at the age of 22. He died, suddenly, in Gran Canaria (learning later from a heart condition). We'd spoke a couple of weeks ago from (his new home in) Brighton. The day before he moved was spent washing his biggish smalls at a launderette in Hulme. Recall every screeching moment but it's only when I see a photo of us outside the laundrette, looking like The Cheeky Girls had let themselves go, that my face finally contorts and I'm consumed with the flames of grief. It's called Dolly Tub Laundry Services, which I'd completely forgotten about. What a name for two scampy camp sisters.

Remember his excruciating talent for puns – his fish tank being home to Goldie-Fish Hawn and Guppi Goldberg, with Gilly (aptly enough) wincing through giggles and telling Scott, "You need your own water-park just to put the name Sea-Lion Dion to use." Remember Scott came round to the flat once, after I'd issued the message: "come over for dinner – we'll endeavour to eat. I'll cook. You bring a bottle." By which I meant a cheap bottle of red or white wine. I open the door to Madam waving a litre bottle of Smirnoff – "Well, that's dinner down the drain. Come in." That night we spoke, for some reason, about death.

"I know what I want played at my funeral," said Scott, "'Single Ladies' by Beyoncé – what do you want played at your funeral?"

"Between my gaggle of gays and the family who'd care to turn up I'll have to find a compromise… rugby with feather boas should do."

"…or fencing with dildos?"

"I'll just have the priest take the bouquet off my coffin and toss it into the crowd to see who's next. That'll warm the room up."

This goes on and on 'til past the bitching hour, cackling with laughter as wide as the world. It's heart-breaking to think he won't retire to the Sandi Toksvig Home for Terminal Punners.

Needing someone, I rush to drench Stevie's shoulder. Though so thin Stevie's arms are bordering on mythical, when he holds me – weeping from quiff to court-shoe – it's like being held by a man mountain. Stevie is often accused of being a depressive, as am I, which is unfair – he's merely a Marilyn Manson fan who knows looking perpetually bored slows down the aging process on the face. My love for him – and our friendship – knows no bounds. On our way to meet Gerry who, dab hand at loss, wishes to join us in raising a sherry for Scott. "Get outta the way, you're in the bike lane!" a cyclist yells, going at his handlebar bell like an AK47. "Of course we are," Stevie yells with death-metal-determination, "we're allowed to be in the bike lane – we're slags! *AND* he's grieving!"

Gerry tells me, "If he's worth crying for he's worth dancing for," and we all dance away into a night, our arched velvet megaphone projection getting us loved and loathed in equal measure.

Socialists by day and lapsed Catholics by night.

Watching the coverage of Tony Benn's death on the news. Remarkable man often referred to as the greatest Prime Minister the country never had. Could listen to his Lady Grey voice all day, an ironed delivery that rests somewhere between fourth martini and severe stroke.

At one point a Channel 4 reporter asks a young man, "So, is socialism important to you, personally?"

"Oh yes, absolutely! I love socialising. It's a very important part of my life."

Resist the pull of a night out and finish reading Suetonius' *The Twelve Caesars*. My favourite sections are Caligula and Nero. Caligula wanted to torture his wife to find out why she loved him so much. People attribute that to caprice, but it isn't; it's the fact that having survived Tiberius (a syphilitic, tired old mare) and his murderousness, he was simply suspicious of devotion that was unconnected to the threat of death. Imagine how exciting that time must have been – when they knew how to do passion.

♦

Suffering through a bout of mannish flu and chained to my duvet. Scroll through emails I haven't checked for weeks and find one from Scott M. sent two days before his death with the message, "Gurl! I've been suspended from Facebook for a month because I accidentally uploaded a photo that was meant for Grindr. Ring me tomorrow – I've got news. X." I laugh, I weep and I raise a glass for another absent friend with an apology to the ether that it took drowning in a river of snot to check my emails.

♦

Visit Phil on my way into town. Need to solemnly bow my head and ask for advice, apropos dating. Though only 23 years old he's something of a well-tanned sexual guru having spent his teenage life being a teenager, rather than a stand-in for a BBC sitcom grandmother. So much so he's only recently purchased his first novel: a gay-themed love story set during trouble-times in Ireland – and, as well as being gay, one of the lovers is Catholic whilst the other is

Protestant. Gripping stuff. Sounds like *Mills & Boon* with balaclavas and nipple clamps, but I ask, "How's the smut rag coming along?"

"Ooh, it's amazing. I were reading it before and it were getting dead racy and I thought to myself 'Phil, you best put this down – you've got a chicken on the stove.'"

Even his non-zingers could floor a humourless cast iron soul.

Tell Phil that after three weeks of dating I'm not sure things are quite working with B. He assures me I'll find the right thing to say and he reminds me: when I dated a fire-breather from Chorley with ADHD, I let him down like a feather, even though he had singed my Joan Crawford eyebrows.

Meet B. in The New Union. I assume our parting will be amicable as we go together like Bonfire Night and epilepsy, but forget he adores more than just a dash of scarf-swishing drama. Tell him it would be nice to be friends, he stares at me for a moment as if he's buffering and then launches into Full Metal Jackie mode.

"I can't believe you – I won't speak to you until you die!"

"Lovely, well we can have a nice chat then." (I don't know why I thought that would help matters.)

"I know where you drink and it's not as if I'm short on offers – everybody wants *me*!"

"How funny you should consider yourself some sort of sex god, as you never once answered my prayers." (Again, I don't know why I thought that would help matters.)

With that he hurls some leaflets about Torremolinos off the nearby bureau and power minces out of the pub. Ring Phil, who seems to think it went very well.

♦

Ann Widdecombe is, once again, complaining about gay marriage – only a few years after so many queens in leotards tried to present her as a cosy Werther's Original-sucking pensioner who, bless her, couldn't dance because of her two far-right feet. I was never fooled. In my opinion she, like Thatcher before her, wants LGBT people gone. Bad hair does not camp make.

After dinner Dad (who is an actor and seasonal Pantomime Dame) rings to tell me that his appearance in the new *Star Wars* film has resulted in him becoming a toy for Christmas 2015. Of course I'm giddy but can't resist. "At last you're going to be a father figure!"

♦

The *Queer Artists of Manchester* calendar, to raise money for the George House Trust, has been retitled *Gays of Manchester* – and is now on sale. My photo is with David H. and Gerry, taken under the gothic romantic glare of John Ryland's Library. Us Three Queens are plastered over August which means retreating to The Outer Hebrides for the summer. Happy to be involved with it but the image used manages to make me look both stern and effete, like some Ewok with an ASBO. Plus, the new title makes it sound like a series of sexy go-go dancers striking coquettish poses – when it's far more a series of filtered mugshots for those who should be shipped off to the Betty Ford clinic. If they'd really wanted to make money for George House Trust they should have sold pink-poppies to commemorate our livers.

Really does feel as if the arts have fallen out of the U.K. Only a few years ago, life for artists living their own mini opera of suburban claustrophobia had a slightly easier time. Now, under the ready-made *Spitting Image* puppet Iain Duncan Smith, any artist without their own chauffeur has already lived longer than they budgeted for. The DWP has made more people homeless than a tsunami, forced the profoundly disabled to pack Quality Street at a B&M in-between chemo sessions and are responsible for so many suicides it resembles nothing less than a class-based genocide. All the Tories are missing is a commission to Hugo Boss for a cabinet uniform.

Never suffered magazine-cover ambition and have lived, quite literally, off my wits for long enough to cover any gin bill, but if I don't find work in the real world soon, I'm at the mercy of Vivaldi. The Job Centre's "on hold" arrangement of his *Four Seasons*, arranged for triangle, recorder and spoon, has been the end of many an artistic endeavour. It really is no wonder the profoundly mentally-ill scream like banshees when they finally get through to Brenda in Great Yarmouth, after a 45-minute wait. Still no word from about handbag towards the short film Kate H. and I wrote (*Golden Balls* – about a gay man riddled with gout and marooned in middle-age, who turns to murdering those younger and prettier. Kate is still convinced it was the "test footage" that got our names scratched off the list of monetary recipients. Footage in which a twink dives into a canal to escape the would-be murderer who – whilst operating his own fog machine – hollers, "I may have tits like cat flaps now – but I was young once. Pretty once! Now, stop waving and start drowning!" I still believe it was our musical number "Prisoner Cell Block HIV" – which was more tasteful than the title suggests.)

◆

Never more aware of living a rather solitary life, no matter how sociable, when it comes to staring at beige-upon-magnolia-upon-beige waiting-room walls. Everybody else up to their rollers in small talk. Desperately trying to block out the creature in lime, turbo chewing gum. There's an old couple: he in scarlet velour tracksuit and grey flatcap, voice like a mouse-fart in a sandstorm; she's all St Tropez glisten and hair dyed the colour of a bin liner. She's already taken over the waiting room, loudly chatting at a handsome Spanish chap who is politely smiling at everything she says.

"He couldn't take his meds this morning (nods towards the husband). Got to be nil-by-mouth. He could murder a cuppa. Couldn't you? He could. He hates swallowing things... Pills... Tablets... Anything. Hates swallowing. Let me tell you cocker, if you don't take the sedation you're a psycho." Cue polite Spanish smile.

Move to yet another waiting room with yet another bead frame toy I've got to pretend not to want to play with. Routine, but dull as Coldplay, endoscopic check-up. The department has been temporarily relocated to a ward reserved for those old enough to look back on their old age. There's a woman nodding off near the TV who, for the fifth time, has woken herself up by breaking wind with alarming ferocity and, for the fifth time, has shot daggers my way then tutted. Another woman shouts, "What is this nonsense?! Put *Bergerac* on!" The channel remains on tennis. A third woman, the only one in lipstick (garish lippy at that) who looks as if she has Waitrose on speed-dial pipes up, "I've not seen Cliff Richard yet... what a cock."

The endoscope itself is vile and I leave feeling like I've been water-boarded. Seemingly this is now life for Guantanamo Gay.

♦

A day so warm the birds aren't trilling but sighing. Too hot to do anything except feel like Blanche Dubois in Primark knickers. Every window and French door in Moston is open, pumping a plethora of TV and radio stations into the streets. It's Lady Gaga next door and Elvis Presley here at number 32. Potter about the house for a few hours, covered with a swamp-like sweat, until Martin messages with an itinerary for chewing the scenery on Canal Street for Gay Pride: "I've got us weekend tickets so start bugle-beading your cardigan." Didn't wish to be in for the long haul but now determined to surpass Martin's friends Glen and David in the trashy stakes of hedonism. Last year they tottered out for Pride on the Friday afternoon and fell in Tuesday morning having done enough ketamine to fell The Grand National. They popped a well-used and very dusty key in the door, whereupon the lock fell out.

Canal Street is a sea of nylon, sequins and Clockwork Tangerine tans. Outside The New Union Pub there's clearly a glitch in the Gay Matrix as we spy four queens in pink Crocs. Feeling faint, Martin and I stagger from macabre discos to Mad Max-style pop-up bars and by 7pm we're tipsy enough to need a breather, so we perch outside The Rembrandt. Sit at a table with two Jewish pensioners in leather hats and harnesses accompanied by their dachshund (also in a tiny leather hat), seemingly all part of a slowly gathering leather fest. Within five minutes it smells like we're drinking inside an inner-tube so we flee to TriBeca where the Irish barman with thighs the size of Bolton can shatter my soul with a smile.

Queuing at the door a cross-eyed woman in a red polka dot dress is asked by the doorman to open her handbag. He takes out a half empty packet of chocolate digestive biscuits and peers inside. "Oh take the biscuits. I'd prefer someone else have 'em or I'll have 'em all." Doorman politely refuses. She then offers the packet to several men, all of whom refuse. "Jesus, what have you got to do to give a digestive biscuit to a gay?!" Reach the front of the queue and the doorman shakes his head, "If you two are together you're barred from here. You ruined that pub quiz for everybody." Memories previously held hostage run wild, "We're bloody glad we did – Gary Barlow was the answer to a science question!" We swish off to play the worst lab rats in the world at a different bar.

In Eagle Bar, struggling to breathe as Martin moulds the indecipherable into the hysterical. Manage to focus in on, what I assume, are four drag queens on the stage singing "C'est la Vie" and comment to Martin, "They're very good – they actually sound just like Bewitched." One of the singers comes slightly off-mic, leans towards me and, barely containing giggles, whispers, "We *are* feckin' Bewitched."

♦

The familiar sight of the Manchester Pride weekend: Canal Street is a wasteland of ketamine skeletons in a fight for the last bottle of water, the disco-damaged are chucking Christmas-cracker-jokes around and the hardened drinkers of the world are searching for a venue where suicidal bar-staff haven't erected a gay-proof safe room. Wearing my hangover like the Mark of Cain I meet the Fag Pack in Paddy's Goose. A reviving hangover sherry and its hairdresser snip-snap-chit-chat as Pearl, Gilly and I exchange "funniest thing overheard at Pride", which is a sort-of race to see whose cringe reflex spasms into concrete first. Some of the best are: "My boss wouldn't let me have Pride off. So I rang him this morning. Told him I've been sectioned and won't get out 'til Tuesday," "I cannot believe he gave me crabs. This is the National Express to Coventry all over again," and "Stick your Jägerbomb, Luke. Sucking up to me will not take back sucking him off."

Pearl leaves first to mentally prepare for spending his last day off putting down lino, Gilly next to put brush to canvas for a new commission and, though as lifeless as a sloth with polio, I meet Stevie and stay out. We've years to come to whittle away sat indoors playing Connect Four and reminiscing about conkers and Dairylea Triangles.

SEPTEMBER – DECEMBER 2014

Left tearful this morning by the nauseating news that Manchester Dogs Home had been set alight by a teenager, who is currently in police custody. Sixty dogs were murdered – and why? Because a young man simply felt like it? Because he had a phobia of rescue dogs who'd already experienced enough human cruelty to give a Victorian millhouse worker a run for her money? Barbara Woodhouse herself wouldn't be able to drill compassion into those guilty of animal cruelty. Those who can murder, or endorse the murder of, animals with such tickle-me-fancy ease can lay no claim to an ounce of humanity. For case in point, Google can quickly whip up photos of the Queen wringing the neck of a pheasant, Prince Harry grinning over the corpse of water buffalo he's shot and David Cameron bragging how he can fell two stags with one shot. It's really little wonder these people can so easily accept poverty and war as a way for others to die by.

♦

Rehearsals with A. go well. Play through two original songs and a cover of Eartha Kitt's "Evil", which I cling onto by the acrylics. When descending into speak-singing there's a fine line between thinking you're baroque Cohen-esque and channelling Benny Hill doing "Ernie (the Fastest Milkman in the West)".

Afternoon drinks at Paddy's Goose are interrupted by someone threatening to jump from the car park facing the pub. The police arrive and the poor queen ends up being talked down but I can't get the image of Kieron, Gilly and I leaping across the bar to turn the radio off as it starting to blare "It's Raining Men" out of my mind. Owen (the barman) later tells us it was to do with a failed relationship. "It was long distance. Those things never work out, do they?" – "I don't know" I answer rather bibulously, "it can do if the three of you trust each other."

♦

Lights are still out on our street. Thank Gloria above for an inexhaustible supply of IKEA tealights Nan picked up in Ashton. At this rate we're looking at the cheapest winter fuel bill in history.

Meet with James for a pot of tea. Only previously met James once. He's an encyclopaedia of unpronounceable science facts, moves with the manic energy of lightning on a bungee rope and is far more "approachable" than me; with the ability to make friends quicker than I lose them. After two pots of tea James, flailing his arms like an octopus trying to retell The Bible through shadow puppets, suggests we move onto alcohol. During the first gin, James is all coy eye-flutters and I realise I'm on a date, so upper lip as sturdy as a bomb shelter I go with it. We drink into the night with the infinite fury of a thousand burning Ford Fiestas and I end up so drunk it takes a 10-minute walk in the sleet of night before I remember my address to order a cab. Invite James back with me. A muffled tryst and we fall comfortably into a lullaby sleep. He gets out of bed in the early hours, assuming to use the toilet but after five minutes or so wonder if he's stood on the landing unsure which door to sprint through. Get up – he's not on the landing, he's not in the bathroom and he's not told me that he sleepwalks. He's wandered downstairs, into the living room where Nan nods off nightly and tried lying down next to her before waking up and rushing out of the room, hands barely covering modesty. Tussling unruly hair, he stresses an exit plan as he cannot face the afternoon-light nods from Nan. Though I can talk to Nan about almost anything this leaves even me a coiled cobra of anxiety, inhaling cigarette after cigarette – filter an' all.

Nan leaves me stewing in my pokey bedroom until 3pm. She must hear my psychic cry for a pot of tea and to my door she ventures. The sonorous knock and I try to levitate my mind into the loft. Hesitate to tell her to come in. The door swings open and she stands, tea-towel in one hand, the other hand on her hip, wearing a mischievous grin; "Well…" (here comes the scolding), "I thought Christmas had come early for *me* last night!" She goes on tell me in microscopic gossip detail about the neighbours. "Margaret was round earlier. She showed me her new bus pass. (Nan purses her lips) She wasn't at all happy with the photo but then she did look a little bit like Elton John on it." The door closes then re-opens to let in a slight of shade, "Don't say anything to your Granddad."

Jessica H. Christ, she's a camp do.

♦

(Having found part-time work in a stationary/art/gift store) Slink into the clunky piece of architecture to dodge another rugby match of housewives battling for Christmas cards and to serve belligerent Wiganer's yelling in anybody's direction about how expensive the wrapping paper is.

Fail to tolerate histrionics and rudeness over the price-hike in Hallmark tack. "Yes, you're quite right – £3.50 for a glittery card is horrific. I'll always remember where I was when I first heard how expensive dancing snowmen toys from overpriced shops are. It's like the Kennedy assassination for my generation. Next!" At this rate I'll be unemployed again before tonight's *Emmerdale*.

A perpetually huffing manager strides over. Orangutang arms violently swinging to display to all her managerial importance. To really hammer the point home she should just beat her chest in front of every Christmas temp like King Kong in an emerald green cardigan and piss on the occasional customer. Told I have to "approach customers" in a "welcoming manner". I tell her I'll need two years at RADA to pull it off and I'm banished to the top floor, which stocks art products and tends to be the quietest of floors.

A well-dressed elderly woman, who has smiled at everyone since she entered the shop, is scanning a table of unfurled posters. She beckons me over and forgoes hello.

"You see this lovely poster of a Vivaldi song sheet?"

"Yes."

"Welllllll, I used it as a backdrop for one of my paintings. I paint, you see."

"Oh yes?"

"Welllllll, I had to trim it down somewhat to fit on one of the lovely canvases you sell here and... welllllll, I didn't notice but a friend recently pointed out that at the top of my painting it now says aldi."

♦

In Liverpool with Jess for the screening of Gerry's documentary. Though, of course, I'm pleased a film-crew have captured Gerry's poetry and life on celluloid I'm not particularly looking forward to seeing my cameo on the silver screen… and I know my best jokes have been cut. Thankfully I have Jess, who boycotted nonsense long ago, to remind me that it isn't my documentary – "One day, Caleb, *perhaps* – but not now."

See the coal-black-coagulation of eye shadow that is Fenella Fielding after the screening of the documentary. Always a delight to be around her and even now, approaching 90, there are few visible Pinewood creaks. Fenella is the closest Blighty ever got to a Grecian siren. One flutter of those mile-long lashes could still bring about a hurricane and those mellifluous tones wrap around any passerby. A whisper becomes a soothing duvet and that smile is an Old School Comedy Revue that, without a word uttered, can make one blush. Who knew I still could... Always beautiful to see her, nostalgia for a time one didn't belong to never creeping far from stage left. An artist who turned down Fellini because she was booked for a gig in Chichester and who wouldn't let a record-breaking sunny day get in the way of wearing her fur-coat. Fur-coat aside it's impossible not to adore and love Fenella. I greet her.

"Darrrrrling," Fenella purrs, "you were wonderful"

"Pardon?"

"In the film. Wonderful – and such beautiful hair too."

Whether silver-tray pleasantry or not I'm tranquilised mute and another talent is added to her long list in the mind. Fenella asks to inspect the badges on the lapels of my jacket. Holding onto my arm she spends a few seconds looking at each one.

"Of course I can't see any of them properly without my glasses." With this she pinches my arm and flashes a wink. Jess remarks, "Fenella Fielding just flirted with you," and I fear I'll never stop smiling.

◆

In work. With a determined gestapo charge a middle aged woman comes straight for me, swinging her M&S bag-for-life with anger that's usually reserved for those who have dated me.

"Oi!"

I scan the floor around my feet. "Ah, there isn't a misbehaving cockier spaniel so you *are* addressing me. Yes?"

"Where are your rulers?!" yelled so viciously it blows the froth of a cappuccino in the adjacent coffee shop.

"My rulers? They're at home."

"Is that meant to be funny?!"

"No. Just grammatically correct until you muster up politeness."

We now have a world so far right and ready for war that politeness can be considered radical behaviour - it's probably the last rebellious act one can commit in the 21st Century, along with not owning a mobile phone.

On my first warning for "speaking back to a customer". Inform management I don't tolerate such things from those I know and if the warning stands by the end of my shift I shall be handing in my notice. The warning is dropped and I march back to tidy pens feeling like Martha Scargill. I must be doing something right, though what I'm not sure.

◆

In the Northern Quarter with Craig P. for a pot of tea. He's just back from working in Glasgow – still the only place I've ever seen someone jogging and smoking at the same time. He seems to have enjoyed it and suggests we visit in the New Year. I agree on the condition he packs footwear more sensible than espadrilles, which he's still wearing as the ghost of Scott of the Antarctic tsks and tuts.

Meet Stevie outside F-A-G Bar. Before our kitten heels can get stuck to a floor that's never been warmly introduced to a bottle of Stardrops we're rejected for "not being regulars". Troll out of the gay village and find ourselves in Retro Bar. The door opens on an almost-empty hovel, stares from the few people stapled near the jukebox, suspicious glances shoot a winter air bottled pre-Moors Murders. Behind the bar there's a camp man standing like an effeminate Quaver which puts us slightly at ease. He introduces himself as Matt and before the Guinness has finished pouring, we've fallen in with who I gather are the rosy-faced irregular regulars.

Stevie whispers a desire for the cherubic-faced bar-tender – who I've a feeling is straight but dare not say anything in case Stevie's disbelief causes him to shriek like a boiling kettle.

"He's so cute. If I could speak to men, he'd be in trouble now."

"Remember sweetheart, no matter how ineffectual a cherub may look they all come equipped with a crossbow and arrow."

He's good looking enough but I don't see what Stevie does – I'm too Jean Genet about men and ultimately desire someone with a criminal record bigger than my quiff.

Two pints of Guinness in and we've found home – it's a grimy, arty, anti-bourgeois paradise. One can hear the ghost of Herbert Huncke mainlining in a cubicle whilst Allen Ginsberg plays the bongos. There's a busty blonde called Ruby held together entirely by tattoos and biker-gang attitude who I enjoy talking to. Stevie is convinced she loathes us, so at least we have something in common for the next time we meet. There's a man with glasses whose name I can't catch but he remembers me from being drunk in Fringe Bar with Mark E. Smith. I don't recall this. His handsome middle-aged punk friend interrupts with that air-raid Mancunian drawl – "Everybody has had a drink with Mark E. Smith – or at least been *in* The Fall. It's like conscription in this city, mate." The Last of the Famous International Mohicans has spoken.

◆

With Nan on her annual North West Christmas market rush. On the list is Aston, Bury, Wigan and, at a push if she's not found suitable tablecloths, Bolton. Today is Harpurhey Market. We have lunch and talk about murder mysteries. These outings could last longer than the DFS sale and I'd never get bored. Get back home to find that Granddad has, quite clearly, fallen in the Christmas tree after a mid-afternoon whisky and passed out on the couch with a cracker in his hair. Nan wakes him up and, after he's stopped blaming the cat, she asks, "Bloody 'ell Frank – Have you broken anything?"

"No I'm fine."

"I meant the presents!"

Contacted by L. about serialising my diaries in an online magazine. Email him back politely declining, telling him that none would care and fewer would read. Besides it isn't quite time and there's little rush. Whatever doesn't kill you only makes your book longer.

Author's Acknowledgements

This chapbook is dedicated to the voices in it who have since joined the feathered choir. Love, always: Paul De Lappe (Pearl), John Grimes, Scott McKinney, Craig Parker, Irene Fletcher (my Great Aunt Rene), Frank Lang (my Granddad) and Sheila Lang (my Nana).

About Superbia Books

Thie Superbia Books imprint was launched with the Superbia Chapbook Competition. The prize was funded by Manchester Pride, and the three winning entries comprise the debut publications under the Superbia Books imprint of Dog Horn Publishing. All three chapbooks were launched as part of Manchester Pride's Superbia strand of arts and cultural events in Greater Manchester. Additional chapbooks were commissioned in 2019 for publication in 2020, including authors local to Greater Manchester.

Additional funding was provided by Commonword in order to mentor the writers, prepare them for publication and organise launch events. Commonword is the literature development agency for the North West.

The editing and mentoring was undertaken by Adam Lowe on behalf of Young Enigma. Founded with seed money from Commonword, Young Enigma supports young and emerging writers from Manchester and the North West.

Find out more at superbia.org.uk, cultureword.org.uk and youngenigma.com.

Superbia Chapbook Series

A Creature of Transformation, James Hodgson
The Moston Diaries, Caleb Everett
Strain, Kenya Sterling
Vivat Regina, Maz Hedgehog

ND - #0130 - 270225 - C0 - 229/152/3 - PB - 9781907133992 - Matt Lamination